KU-244-262

THE EMPEROR'S WATCHMAKER

by
Lemn Sissay

illustrated by
Gail Newey

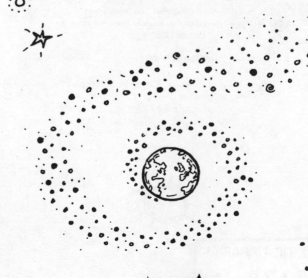

BLOOMSBURY
CHILDREN'S
BOOKS

For Abiyu, Wuleta, Stephanos, Mimi,
Mehatem, Tsahaiwork and Teguest

All rights reserved; no part of this publication may be reproduced or
transmitted by any means, electronic, mechanical, photocopying or otherwise,
without the prior permission of the publisher

First published in Great Britain in 2000
Bloomsbury Publishing Plc, 38 Soho Square, London, W1V 5DF

Copyright © Text Lemn Sissay 2000
Copyright © Illustrations Gail Newey 2000

The moral right of the author has been asserted
A CIP catalogue record of this book is available from the
British Library

ISBN 0 7475 4755 6

Printed in Great Britain by Clays Ltd, St Ives plc

10 9 8 7 6 5 4 3 2 1

DUDLEY PUBLIC LIBRARIES

L   45329

G16781   SCH

J 821 SIS

Contents

Welcome!   7
Birds of the Palace Library   8
The Emperor's Proclaimer   10
When I'm Older   12
The Man on the Moon   14
The Prince of Toffee   16
Donizetti and the Cat Juggler   18
The Princess's Laugh   20
The Emperor's Butterfly Maker   22
Lulu the Emperor's Dog   23
The Palace Parrot   26
The Emperor's Cat   27
Body Language   30
The Bedroom from Hell   32
The Ghost that Makes Breakfast   34
Wouldn't it Be Great!   38
I'm Sorry I'm Sorry I'm Sorry   40
The Murky Land of Smo   41
Roundabout Roundabout   44
Left Out!   46

Pass it on   47

Oh Fantastic Chip   48

Excuses Excuses   50

She Read as She Cradled   52

The Perky Palace Pigs   54

Daydreams   55

Everything is Rhythmical   56

The Broken Biscuit Thief   58

The Emperor's Watchmaker   60

The Prince Who Has No Family   62

Everything is Still   63

Welcome!

whoosh!

Welcome to words
The wonderful world of words
Where stampeding herds (of words)
Whizz through the wind
There they go
Passwords and last words
The lost words of crosswords
No scare words just bywords
All of them my words

Fierce flocks of fly words
Deep words going skywards
Goodbye and Hi words
Poke in the eye words
Overheard words
Here words and there words

Welcome to words
The wonderful world of wordy
Wicked wild worldy winding
Wishful whizzing whacky words!
Whoosh!

w   w   i
o   o   s
n   o
d   s   h   f
e   h   u
r   i
f   n   l
u   g   .
l   .   w
.   w   o
w   o   r
o   r   d
r   d   s
s   .
.   .
.   .
.   .
.   .
.

Birds of the Palace Library

The books in the library are folded birds.
Neatly, in rows they pretend to sleep,
Wings tucked tidily to their sides
But with one eye lightly and slightly open
They dream, as you walk past the ledges
You'll stroke them, hold them in your palms
And unfold their weathered wings.
They're the birds of imagination made by writers
    like me
So open them up! Open them up – set the colony
    free!

Let them fly. When they do they'll whisper to you
Before you know it your feet will leave the ground.
And warm rushes of air will brush against your skin
You are soaring amongst a flock of beating wings
You are flying, gliding, sliding through the sky.

The books in the library are folded birds.
They will raise you higher than you could imagine
And carry you back to the library as if you'd never
  gone
Then they land gracefully upon their ledges
Sit quietly on their edges
And wait patiently for the next passer by to sigh
To stand by a bird with its half opened eye.
Its gentle bird-heart beating hoping to be opened.

This is why libraries are silent. So not to disturb
  the birds.
Whisper ... don't startle the others
Look at us. Look. Thousands of us waiting for you.
We are the birds of imagination from a place you
  cannot see
So open us up! Open us up up up up up up up up up up

The Emperor's Proclaimer

He swished through the crowd at The Square
With his rose of a nose held high in the air
(The proclaimer loved the attention there
And made much of such a simple affair)
He held the lapels of his velvet coat
Stroked his hair, cleared his throat

He was a ship of a man rich with catch
Two jangling lifeboats of fat attached.
His body quivered from chin to hips
As a bolshy burp burst from his lips
He sniffled his nostrils, raised his chubby chin
Glared at the grubby people staring at him

Then he read out his list with bulging eyes
'Clean up the streets and brush the skies'
He'd say 'Tidy the mountains put away the sheep
If the fields look tatty, sweep sweep sweep
Then polish the rocks and dust off the clouds
Silence the rivers – they're too loud'

With a twiddle of his tash, a sniff of his snout
A flick of his eye and a hint of a pout
With a short snort he'd tuck away his scroll
Turn and return to his stroppy little stroll
Saying 'I am the proclaimer as you all knows
And whatever I says is whatever is goes'

11

When I'm Older

I'll never pull my socks up. I'll never fold my clothes
I'll even have a servant to wipe my drippy nose
And at the dinner table FIRST I'll have my sweet
I'll always rush my tea and never brush my teeth

I'll never wipe my face and never clean my shoes
I'll never cry never ever. I'll never flush the loo
I'll never do my homework. I'll never eat sprouts
When Mum asks 'where you going' I'll say 'OUT'

I'll never clean my bedroom, never change my socks
I'll always yell 'OI!' through the letterbox
I'll never wash the pots. I'll never do my bed.
For breakfast I'll only eat jam on shortbread

I'll never wipe my feet, I'll never wipe my nose
I'll never cut my nails and I'll never wash my clothes
I'll always ring the doorbell, I'll never wear a tie
I'll always answer the telephone with the word
                                        Goodbye!

The Man on the Moon

He collects the white bits of daylight
Shuffles them into his pockets
And wellington boots
Down his pants and
In the lining of his suit

He scrapes daylight from leaves
Wet from the rain.
Licks it off windows.
And with a small spoon he'd scoop it
From the edges of shadows

He'd put three mirrors
At the foot of his house
And each and every morning
He would strip the sunrise from the mirrors
And catch some more by yawning

Then he'd race to each doorstep
And take the bottle tops
Tiptoe through the gate
Run into the valley
And skim the sun from the lake

But his real work begins
In the darkest night
This is when he flies
To a heart-shaped rock
In the middle of the sky

He takes the sun from out his pockets
All the bottle tops and silver lockets
He pulls his arm right back
And throws it back into the black
Like fireworks it sprays the midnight gloom
The light at night is from the man on the moon

The Prince of Toffee

You haven't heard what the boy said
The boy whose palace was made of toffee
Who ate three boxes of chocolates each day
And has thirty sugars in each cup of coffee?

Whose palace walls are chocolate bricks
And whose windows have marzipan ledges
The flagpole, of course, is a liquorice stick
And in the garden there are candyfloss hedges

The moat is awash with creamy milk shake
And the drawbridge made from caramel
On the tops of the walls sugared fruits and all
Have you ever had such a heavenly smell?

But you haven't heard what the prince said
The boy who was to become king
The boy who ate sherbet for breakfast
Melted toffee ice-cream and doughnut rings?

The boy with bed sheets made of icing.
Whose pillows are slices of Battenberg cake
Whose water from the taps is Coca Cola
And in his grounds a Vimto lake

His garden is dotted with coconut macaroons
That sparkle with a sugary lip-licking light
Even the morning dew is treacle and honey
With star drops dropped down from the night

People travel from miles to see him
And when asked – 'Child! Don't you miss meat?'
He would lick a wall and smile at them all.
'But life is sweet' he replied, 'Life is sweet.'

And a smile so wide bounced from ear to ear
And the crowd drew breath at what was seen
For he had no teeth except one
That was proud, slanted and green.

Donizetti and the Cat Juggler

My grandma, Grandma Rossetti
Sits up all night and knits spaghetti
Says it's for the her friend the Yeti
Whose name is Donizetti
He's music to her ears (she calls him 'dear')
But he never appears whenever I'm near
'Donizetti' she shouts loud and clear
I turn but quick as mountain deer
Donizetti disappears
'He'll be back later' she whispers
'When you're not here'

Once she knitted a bathtub and a house
A woolly jumper for my pet mouse.
She's going to knit a ladder, she says, to the stars
She tried knitting a car but didn't get far
Once she knitted a camel jumper
With holes cause it was a two humper.
And Day-Glo earmuffs for a freezing hare
And prime ministerial mittens for Cherie Blair.
But wait before you think that's mad
You haven't met me grandad!

Now Grandad Illuminati both clever and arty
Is teaching himself the art of karate
While juggling our three scrawny cats
Who were not born to be acrobats
They hurtle and spin they dip and they dive
Their ears shoot up (they're glad they're alive)
Their startled eyes spin round and their tails curl
Four legs point to four corners of the world
They twirl in air like astronauts in space
With 'help me' written across each face
In cat language they say 'put me down'
When Grandad does they sulk and frown
Legs go wobbly, eyes go cross-eyed
Then all three fall flat upon their sides

I am just warning you before the visit
That it's not normal to be like this, is it?
But the truth is at the end of the day
I wouldn't want them any other way!
Cause no one can knit spaghetti for a Yeti
Like my great grandma Rossetti
And if you ever see someone juggle cats
You know my grandad first did that

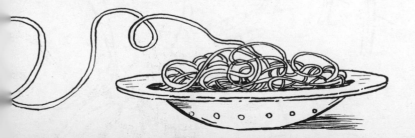

The Princess's Laugh

When the princess laughs in class, miss
Her head spins round and round
She jiggles about so much, miss
Her tiara slips right down

Her desk shakes and shivers, miss
It's like a giant boom
When the princess laughs in class, miss
It takes over the whole room

Her head flips back, her black hair dances
And her lips open so far
That the whole class could climb in, miss
And you, miss, could park your car

Her mouth gets so wide her tonsils hang down
Like two gorillas enjoying a dance
And, miss, her laugh is so loud
They can hear it in the cafés of France.

Then she goes quiet for a second, miss
Hand on mouth she tries to hold it in
But, miss, that just makes it worse, miss
Cause she starts us all laughing

If there is an earthquake in China
(I know this sounds daft)
But I can guarantee (believe you me)
The princess has laughed!

The Emperor's Butterfly Maker

I work at the butterfly-making factory
On Butter Lane in a town called Fly
Near a city called Flower.
Every day I stick on the wings
And watch them flit from my fingers.

Their wings sound like cats purring
As they lilt and loop away
Maybe I'll try the wings myself
One day.

Lulu the Emperor's Dog

Lulu was the emperor's dog, *the* dog
More than a mutt-mongrel or palatial pet
With his fine hair and long neck
Never a better model for a statuette.

He had airs did Lulu and graces too
His tail raised like a golden fan in the air
As he tiptoed on perfect padded paws
Past the door-man and commissionaire.

His eyebrows were raised and his eyes sparkled
He was a high-brow dog in his prime
He'd eat with a knife and fork if he could
And a serviette at dinner time

His face was sprayed with the best perfume
Nails manicured by the finest beautician
Eyebrows plucked with golden pincers
And his hair washed and, of course, conditioned

By day he would trot by the emperor's side
Or walk in the grounds to survey the land
And meet city-cats and discuss Baudelaire,
Albert Camus, Rossetti, or Bertrand

Lulu was a Japanese breed but a lion of mind
No more than four paws tall
With hair so fine in golden waves
Like a miniature waterfall

But don't be fooled by style and grace
The mere smell of an unwanted intruder
Would stop him in his tracks, he'd turn his neck
And show gnashers like a barracuda

The fine hair would bristle upon his back
His roar would echo through town
One robber was so scared his clothes ran away
Till all he wore was a frown

But Lulu liked to play – as dignitaries stood
He'd flip gently in the air right over his back
But nobody dared to say a word
Cause it was the emperor's dog was that

The Palace Parrot

The palace parrot copied everything I said
The palace parrot copied everything I said

If I said I am stupid
Guess what the parrot said

If I said you are stupid
Guess what the parrot said

If I said you are brilliant
Guess what the parrot said

If I said you are beautiful
Guess what the parrot said

If I said you are wonderful
Guess what the parrot said

If I said I'll do anything for you
Guess what the parrot said

Oh. Thank you very much.

The Emperor's Cat

I'm a sonic superstylish
Cool kind of cat
I wear my own fur coat
and matching fur hat

I got a white Nike streak
All the way down my back
And I got milk from the palace
On tap! You got that

I'm no stray-cat, alley cat
No rat-catching, scally cat
I'm no back-scratching, dilly-dally cat
I'm the cat – you got that

I like the fine things
I eat caviar, only sleep on silk
Only use chauffeur-driven cars
I only drink premium milk

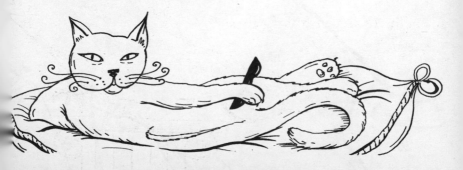

When I need exercise
I send the butler out for a jog
Lulu may be a nice canine
But this cat is the top dog

You get what I'm saying here
The emperor is nice, so's his wife,
But he can't catch a mouse
To save his life

They be screaming and hollering
Stood on the table top
And they don't call the butler
Nor that crazy lazy dog

I walk into their room
On hearing all this fuss
I stare that mouse in the eye
'This palace ain't big enough for two of us'

I use my hip hypnosis
Get that mouse in a daze
I say 'You are feeling sleepy
So get outa my paLACE (ahem)'

And off it goes, just like that
Cause I am a class act
I'm hypnotic and supersonic
I'm THE cat – you got that.

Fact. I'm the prime minister
Of cats a class act, got that fact
I'm Action packed. Government backed
I'm THE cat – you got that.

Body Language

My legs keep running away
And one hand won't talk to the other
My left foot says she's fallen out
With her outrageous brother

My elbow says it's sick of bending
In the direction of my arm
My shoulder says it's got an itch
And there are no trees in my palm

My stomach says it's angry
And has started sticking out
It says it's sick of being inside
And really wants to be out

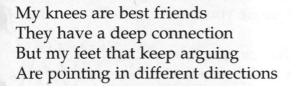

My ears have started flapping
They want to be wings
And my hair has gone straight up
Cause it couldn't see anything

My knees are best friends
They have a deep connection
But my feet that keep arguing
Are pointing in different directions

My eyes have argued again
And refuse to work in time
And my bottom says it's sick
Of always being behind!

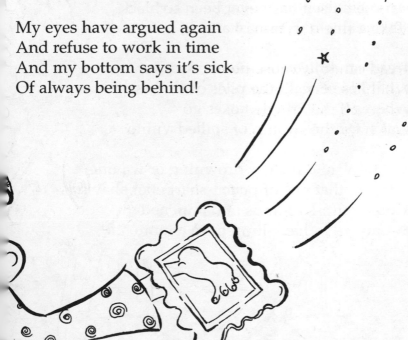

The Bedroom from Hell

Welcome to the BEDROOM FROM HELL
Hear, as you enter, the low church bell
Cover your nose from the horrible smell
And wear gloves cause you never can tell.

And bring a torch because without that
You'll never ever find your way back
Darkness itself has never been so black
(Take a shield in case of attack)

Tread carefully cause no one knows
What lies beneath the piles of clothes
Where all the Pringle boxes go
Watch for the swamp of spilled Vimto

Maybe a child neither drowning or waving
Is lost in that pile of pencil-sharpener shavings
Mouldy murky lumps of dampened
Sweaty socks hang limp from a lamp and

The window is streaky with dust and with dirt
On the inside ledge there's a manky shirt
A rat emerges from its cuffs and snuffles as rats do
If you don't clean your bedroom this could be you.

An old mechanical doll circles a cup
See that skeleton – it used to be a pup
Poor pet, never even got to see his way.
Since he entered the bedroom from hell that day.

Posters on the walls of the footballers shout
No. They scream. Let me out, let me out
They never knew! They never could tell
That this bedroom is the
BEDROOM FROM HELL

The Ghost that Makes Breakfast

As shadows fight in the dead of night
For space by light of the candle
I hear again the larder door
The turn of its springy handle
My eyes, like a page, flick open
From the short chapter of sleep.
And I hear the whine of the larder
And the shuffle of tired old feet

Stepping from my bed, half awake
I stub my toe on the floor
And while hopping in pain, hit my head
Upon the hardwood bedroom door.
Ow! Shhhhh! I fold my lips over teeth
And moan in part pain and part fear
I couldn't let a sound burst out, not here
For fear that the ghost might hear

I slid down the banister of the stairs
A silent helter-skelter ride
And landed just like Batman on the hall floor
Dizzy and slightly cross-eyed.
At the end of the hall, from the kitchen door
A light only slightly spilled through
I hid against the wall and walked towards it
Like the Egyptians do.
The frizzle and sizzle of the frying pan
Got louder and louder with every step
And the bubbling of something in a large pan
Made a curl of sweat skim down my neck.
I peeked through the crack in the door
A silver knife raised higher than my head
Chopped down hard and strong
Through freshly baked granary bread.

But no one was holding the knife
It must have been AN INVISIBLE GHOST
And I am sure I heard the whispered words
'Do you like jam upon your toast'
Next eggs were juggling in a circle
Popping themselves into the bubbling pan
A waterfall of Frosties spilled into bowls
And beans poured themselves from the can

Strings of sausages hung above the stove
Like a snake charmer's favourite trick
And laid themselves in a circle on the fat
And rocked so they wouldn't stick.
The fridge door opened and threw out its light
Tinkling bottles of orange juice floated politely by
And poured perfectly into tall glasses
I couldn't believe my eyes.
By now I was sat on the stool by the table
And watched this happen around me
The wonderful whirlpool of milk butter
Knifes forks and toast floating around me
Miniature seagulls of salt passed my brow
And spread themselves on the eggs
A spit of fat jumped from the pan
But disappeared before it hit my leg

I slept that night happy in the knowledge
Of the secret that I had found
It's a ghost that makes the breakfast for us all
That lays the table without a sound
The next morning I told Father, who laughed at me
But in seeing that I was serious said 'Look.
It doesn't matter that she is invisible at all.
She's a wonderful cook!'

So if you come home and the food is ready
And you are not sure how it was made
Ask your mother or father if it was the ghost
There's no need to be afraid
And, like I do, say thank you.
As I say thank you to the ghost.
Now every morning when I go for my breakfast
She spells my name in the jam on the toast.

Wouldn't it Be Great!

It'd be great if stamp-licking left a tang on the tip
Of the tongue – a trace of the taste of tropical fruit.
If you didn't have to go down the stairs each morning
Because it was more fun to run and then parachute.
It'd be great if tears curled and swirled not down
To the world but up, up and away to the sky
Reflecting the colours of the sunset perfecting
As they fly – wings waving goodbye

It'd be great (I tell you) to paint the grey town
Turquoise and turmeric like a grand colouring book
It'd be great if something was given for everything took
If something was loosened for everything stuck
It'd be great to turn down the growling sound
Of the crawling cars and turn up the tone of the trees
To sing jazz solos with swooping swallows
And discuss the bizz with the buzz of the bees

It'd be great to grow grapes from light sockets
And orange orchids from my inside pockets
And to sleep deep in the curve of a picture locket
Then swerve to school on my personal jet rocket
Cause I'd go faster and faster and I'd never stop it
I'd go over chimney pots and mountain tops
I'd return to school, right there I'd swap it
One jet rocket for one sweetshop. (He-he)

I'm Sorry I'm Sorry I'm Sorry

It was the way you stopped – mid laugh
The moment I said it I knew I shouldn't have
I didn't mean to say it. Not the way that I did
I didn't mean it – the way it sounded
What I mean is I said it but the wrong way round
When I said it I read it again in your frown
It shouldn't have come out, I should have kept it in
Not that it was in if you see what I am saying
I'm sorry I'm sorry I'm sorry. What I mean to say is
    I regret it
I pushed it over the edge, I did. I sensed it when I
    said it

The Murky Land of Smo

Smo was a beautiful land
A beautiful land of tears
Its king was a horrid man
Who'd kept it in chains for years

Smo had become so dry
That the rain was black ash
The rivers were polluted
Black was the colour of the grass

The ash covered the birds
And almost everything
There was only winter it seemed
No summer, no spring

The whole country smelt dank
It was so thick with fog and tar
That nobody ever saw a sun
The moon or a single star.

There were shadows by day
And shadows by night
And all anyone wanted
Was a little bit of light.

Then a small girl in Smo heard
Of the fresh flowers of spring
She said that one day she'd
Stop the horrid Smo King

So she shouted from hilltops
Until everybody did sing
Stop the Smo King, Stop the Smo King
Stop the Smo King, Stop the Smo King

She shouted from her front room
She shouted loud and clear
'Stop the Smo King'
So everyone could hear

She shouted in the night-time
She shouted in the day
'Stop the Smo King
Stop the Smo King – okay!'

She shouted until
The Smo King had stopped
And the misty air lifted and the
The Smo King had dropped

The ash blew away
And the rivers turned fair
And spring flowers bloomed
Just about everywhere

Until people saw the sun
The stars and everything
And always remembered the little girl
Who had stopped the Smo King.

Roundabout Roundabout

I like the way water swoops ROUND the plug hole I like all the circles of cream inside a swiss roll I sit aROUND the fire and eat ROUND fruit on a ROUND plate I'll tell my mate I'll be ROUND at aROUND about 8 I like the way water swoops ROUND the plug hole I like swerves and swirls I sit aROUND the fire and eat ROUND garden aROUND me Everything is ROUND!! The stars The world I like curls I like swerves and swirls I sit aROUND castle with a ROUND garden aROUND me Everything is ROUND!! The stars The world I live in a ROUND tea I live in a ROUND castle with a ROUND I eat ROUND biscuits and dip them in my ROUND tea I live in a ROUND

You wouldn't believe how good ROUND feels I even drive a ROUND car with ROUND wheels I go ROUND the ROUNDabout aROUND and aROUND I even like the way ROUND sounds ROUND bubbles ROUND balloons ROUND and ROUND and ROUND I like bends I like curves I like swoops and swerves They send ROUND my head I like bends I like curves I see the ROUND moon (through ROUND eyes) in my ROUND bed I have ROUND dreams and I wake At the perfect time aROUND ROUND about it!

45

Left Out!

You call me an odd sock
But I'm sick of being called odd
Just because I like to go my own way

How would you like
To have a sweaty foot shoved
Down your mouth all day

Pass it on

Tell Brian to tell Jane to tell Janine
to tell Germaine to tell June to tell Maxine
Tell Linda to tell Lucinda to tell Mel
to tell Genet to tell Mesrat to tell Del
to tell Ashraf to tell Akin to tell Jimmy
to tell Nadia to tell Nazreen to tell Timmy
to tell Lynn to tell Jim to tell Anne
to tell Jill to tell Joane to tell Jan
to tell Joe to tell Jack to tell John
that I'm not talking to him or anyone!

Oh Fantastic Chip

Within my firm forked grip
The chip slips towards my lips
In all its golden gorgeous glaze
I ask for chips on all days.

This salted sire of this sight of style
This brightly lit golden mile
My darling deep-fried friend.
Our love shall never end

This crispy crunchy perfect coat
Oh salted sailing oblong boat
This log of love. Oh! po-ta-to
Dipped into sauce du to-ma-to

This friend of food, pal of the plate
My royal loyal best mate
I've said enough and cannot wait
For you the chip are near your fate

Though, my dearest, our love lasts
Alas there's nothing more I can do
Than stick you in my gob
And chew and chew and chew!

Adieu, my love, adieu.

Excuses Excuses

When you don't want a bath

There's a shark in the bath. There's a shark in
    the bath
And it's not funny! And it's not a laugh!
It's true I tell you, there's a shark in the bath

When you don't want to go to bed

There's an elephant in my bed, there's an elephant
    in my bed
And I am not telling lies. It's not in my head.
I promise it's true. There is an elephant in my bed

When you don't want to clear the table

There's a buffalo in the kitchen, a buffalo in
    the kitchen
And it's not a web of lies that I'm stitching
I promise it's true there's a buffalo in the kitchen

When you don't want to go to the toilet

There's a pig on the loo, I say a pig on the loo
And I am not telling lies, what I say is true
I promise, I promise there's a pig on the loo

When you don't want to switch the light off

There's a monkey on the light, a monkey on the light
It's eating a banana. I promise that I'm right
I swear a monkey's swinging on the light

There's a monkey on the light, shark in the bath
But Mum just looks at me, she's about to laugh
Yes she says and pigs might fly
And behind her through the window a flock fly by.

She Read as She Cradled
(What the empress said as the princess slept)

You part of me

Every day your history
Every tomorrow your destiny
Every growth your mystery
Every mother wants a baby
        Like you

Every laugh your personality
Every look your clarity
Every word your stability
Every mother wants a baby
        Like you

Every hiccup a comedy
Every fall a catastrophe
Every worry my worry
Every step you're beside me
Every sight you're pure beauty
Every mother wants a baby
                    Like you

Every tear wiped carefully
Every word spoke lovingly
Every meal fed silently
Every cloth washed caringly
Every song sung sweetly

Every day I whisper quietly
Every mother wants a baby
                    Like you

The Perky Palace Pigs

The two pink portly pigs had decided
They weren't talking to each other
And were ignoring each other
Trying not even to see each other
They simply didn't agree with each other
They pottered around each other
And uttered not a sound to each other
They slept in hay opposite each other
Facing always away from each other
They would never sit with each other
When the farmer called them each one
They trotted out one by one
Their snouts facing away from each other
With nothing at all to say to each other
'It's bacon tomorrow' said the farmer
His face as worn as old leather
So quickly the two pigs became friends again
And ran away together.

Daydreams

Daydreams float into me
Without my even knowing
I feel myself drift away
Don't know where I'm going

I glide through the window
And drift above the crowds
I sail into the milky sky
And slip above the clouds

A daydream just happens
Nobody can plan it
It's nature's way of making me
Fly above the planet

But a noisy spaceship passes
It looks like it's going to break up
My teacher's inside it screaming
Wake up Wake up WAKE UP!

Everything is Rhythmical

Rhythm rhythm
Can you
Hear the
Rhythm

Quick rhythm
Slick rhythm
God given
Life livin

Rhythm rhythm
Can you
Hear the
Rhythm

If you listen close
Ears to the ground
The bass of noise
Is rhythm's sound
From spoken word
To ways of walk
From rap to reggae
And funk we talk (in)

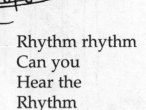

Rhythm rhythm
Can you
Hear the
Rhythm

Way back in the heart of Africa
They took our drums away
But rhythm proved its own power
By being here today

All four corners sweet-sounding rhythms reach
With treble in the speaker, even bass in speech
From the freezing cold to heat in heights
Mohammed Ali did use it in his fights

With

Quick rhythm
Slick rhythm
Gold rhythm
Bold rhythm
God given
Life livin

Rhythm rhythm
Can you
Hear the
Rhythm

The Broken Biscuit Thief
(Written by B. Ourbon.)

A biscuit's gone missing from the kitchen
'It's no laughing matter' growled the judge
'Crumbs have been found and your napkin
Has a very biscuity smudge –

'We've counted the ones in the tin' he said
'Here's the picture.' He showed me the proof
'We have a recording of it opening' he smirked
'From a camera we hid on the roof'

'I'm innocent' I cried from the dock
'I didn't touch the biscuits' I said
'Take him away' barked the judge
'And feed him nothing but bread.'

So they took me down to the dungeons
And just before I fell into dreams
I heard the crunch in my pocket
Of a secret single gypsy cream

Never has a biscuit tasted so good
In all its sugary delight
As I saw the moon like a biscuit
Hanging in the sky at night

For I AM the biscuit thief
I stole the gypsy creams
And I sleep well in my cell tonight
Within my biscuity dreams.

The Emperor's Watchmaker

	tic
toc	
	tic
toc	
I am the watchmaker	tic
The Emperor's watchmaker toc	
And to make sure he's on time	tic
I finish my lines toc	
With a tic or a toc	tic
In case his watch stops toc	
If he trips on his sock,	tic
Or drops a stitch toc	
Or falls from the rocks	tic
I never let one slip toc	
I never let one drop	tic
I don't slip or lose grip toc	
I don't stop	tic
Quick from the lip toc	
Steady as a rock	tic
If I feel like being poetic toc	
Or cook in a pot or wok	tic
Even when I am sick toc	
Even when I'm not	tic
Even when I dream I stick toc	

to the tictoc   tic
And the toctic   toc
Cause I am the Emperor's watchmaker   tic
And I can't stop it   toc
The Plot. The Plot   tic
   tic
toc
   tic
toc-toc
    tic-tic
toc-toc-toc-toc
    tic-tic-tic-tic-tic

The Prince Who Has No Family

The prince who has no family watches all the others,
Sisters with brothers and fathers with mothers,
And he watches how they touch and they shout
And he watches them stay still and fall out
Catching buses and trains and taxis and planes
The prince who has no family stands in the rain

The prince who has no family watches the others,
Sisters with brothers and fathers with mothers,
He watches them laugh and sometimes cry
He watches them grow and sometimes die
He watches them coo and watches them call
He watches them doing things and nothing at all

The prince who has no family watches the others,
Sisters with brothers and fathers with mothers,
He watches old hands holding young hands
And sees their footsteps pepper their sand
He watches them argue and wishes it was true
That he had someone to argue with too

Everything is Still

The cat curled cautiously in a corner
And the dog dozed on the doormat.
The pets slept as the maid swept
The clock clicked and toc ticked
All the dot-to-dots have been done
And all the colouring in has been filled
And all the games played are won
And everything is still.

As if the looming moon itself did cry
Snow slipped from the sloping sky
And limboed under the lamplight
A flock of white butterflies by night
They weave their way through wind
And rest upon home and hill
And melt into everything
'Til everything is still.

The darling buds of day are done
The leaping loop of light is run
Now sleeps the blue sky and its sun
With nothing lost and nothing won
The mist lies upon the quiet crops
And the wind sleeps on the windowsill
And the moon rests on the roof-tops
And everything is still . . .

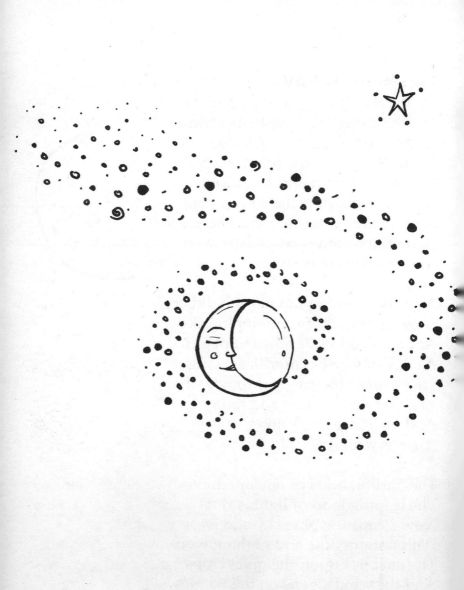